SECRETS TO RUNNING A SUCCESSFUL BUSINESS

(How To Have FUN Getting More Business)

Angelica Rose
The Heart Of Motivation

**Secrets To Running A Successful Business
(How To Have Fun Getting More Business)**

Angelica Rose

The Heart Of Motivation
email: angelica_rose@cheerful.com or
angelica1rose@yahoo.com
website: http://angelicarose.freeyellow.com

Page Design, Typesetting and Editing:
      Cat & Mouse Design (206) 246-7105

Photography by:
      Eagle Portrait, Inc.
      (206) 242-9565

Printing by:
      Lithtex Printing Solutions
      Stephanie Moe 503-641-5367

Library of Congress Catalog Card Number:
      93-73975

Rose, Angelica
      Secrets to running a successful business: how to have fun
      getting more business / by Angelica Rose

Published by JLR Publishing

ISBN 0-9639304-0-0

Printed and bound in the United States of America

Acknowledgments

Special thanks to the following:

God
(Keep the Faith.)

Darren Peck, James Cox, and Carlos Hart
Eagle Portrait, Inc.

Lithtex Printing Solutions
Stephanie Moe

Warren D. Smith, CPC - Integrated Marketing

Bill Huenefeld - Small Business Development Center

Linda Frazee - Positive Imagery

Steve Gersman

Burr Burrell and Sally & Jim Bartz - Dale Carnegie & Associates

Mom and Dad Bogart

Bonnie Ermillio and Neil Bogart

Family
Thanks Dad, for caring enough to make my life better

Gain company profitability and customer service by developing your greatest asset — YOUR PEOPLE.

Angelica Rose
The Heart Of Motivation

Gain Company Profitability + Customer Satisfaction By Empowering Staff Personally and Professionally

Success = (Company Profitability + Customer Satisfaction) X (People)

cash flow	customer service	skills
inventory control		self belief
healthy sales	new customer cost	positive attitudes
accounts receivable	vs.	goals
accounts payable	satisfying existing customers	

Create Win Win Win Success!

Company	**Customers**	**Staff**
happier staff	product/service satisfaction	job satisfaction
higher productivity	efficient delivery of requests	more enthusiasm
greater personal &	enhanced communications	high motivation
professional rewards	meet own deadlines	better attitudes
more bottom line projects		improved teamwork
Customer and market driven		enriched personal life
existing customer referrals		

Company Profitability and Customer Satisfaction Are Multiples Of What Your *People* Do!

Mission Statement

Angelica Rose's Mission Statement is based on the notion that:

Anything we choose to achieve in life — whether it be Success, Profit, or Satisfaction — is created by our relationship with oneself and with others.

Angelica uses a unique combination of intuitive, creative, & leadership skills as a motivational speaker, personal coach and business consultant since 1984. She tailors the talks to the audience and holds the participants accountable for the results. She uses a variety of media, including radio, television, newspapers, and numerous publications.

Table of Contents

Are We Having Fun Yet?

Chapter 1

Plan Your Work and Work Your Plan.

- How to have fun while working smart.

Chapter 2

A Destructive Mind Is A Wonderful Thing To Lose.

- Conquering it all and feeling alive as you break old habits, fears, and limited thinking patterns that don't work.
- More rainbows beyond your dark clouds.
- Get more energy, enthusiasm, and self-confidence.
- Feeling like you are valued, respected, and worthwhile.

Chapter 3

Motivation: What Makes You and Your Customers Go?

- Knowing where you are going and getting what you want once you get there.
- Live in the present and the future will take care of itself.
- Feel the vitality of life's abundance of riches.

Chapter 4

How To Get the Business

- Discover the diamonds in the rough.
- Secrets of the hidden treasure.
- Get paid what you are worth.

Chapter 5

Making the Sale: Doing It By the Numbers.

- How to determine if your prospect is qualified for sale or for unemployment.
- Learn the secrets of gaining one's attention.
- Discover the emotional reasons for buying using 3 areas to question.
- Give "knock them dead" presentations that make your customers want to buy.
- Get objections to get sales.

Chapter 6

Increase Sales and Keep Your Customers Satisfied!

- Increase your client base without hitting the pavement (literally).
- Happy customers = happy salespeople.
- Relate to your customers before they relate to your competitors.
- We're all in the same boat, so clean up your act.
- Building effective relationships makes you feel appreciated and respected.
- It ain't over until the customers are happy and the paper work is done.
- Just one more thing: who do you know that I want to know?

Chapter 7

Do Your Taxes or You May Be A Jailbird.

- Prepare your taxes properly before the IRS takes care of it for you.

Preface

We all want to be successful in our life endeavors. Success can be defined as having financial profitability for some people and as a satisfied feeling of accomplishing dreams for another.

This book defines success in a formula comprised of 3 components: (Profits + Customer Satisfaction) X People. The more people develop their skills, attitudes, self-image, and goals, the more profits and customer satisfaction is enhanced — thus, more enriched success. In this book, you will learn what it takes to run a successful business.

"Formula for Success"

By Angelica Rose

Gain Company Profitability + Customer Satisfaction By Empowering Staff Personally and Professionally

Success = (Company Profitability + Customer Satisfaction) X (People)

cash flow	customer service	skills
inventory control		self belief
healthy sales	new customer cost	positive attitudes
accounts receivable	vs.	goals
accounts payable	satisfying existing customers	

- Tools to enrich your communication and listening skills.

- Ways to establish satisfied customers for repeat business.

- Improved customer relations.

- Where and how to increase your clientele.

- Ways to run a smoother business operation avoiding unnecessary costly mistakes and more!

Cycle of Development

Skill
(success)

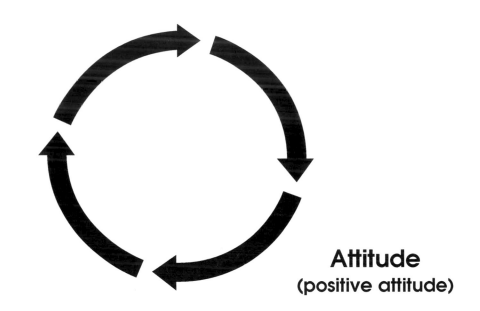

Practice
(mistakes)

Attitude
(positive attitude)

Knowledge
(written and verbal information)

Chapter

1

Business Plan

Every successful business has a business plan. A business plan helps you to get focused on the proper steps for starting a business. To keep the business operating efficiently, the business plan is constantly revised over time as market and customer needs change. The business plan is also used to check on performance over time. It consists of the following components:

Name of your business

Legal structure

Target market

Competition

Market strategy

Financial planning

Business operation

In the following pages, you will find an elaborate outline of a business plan.

Outline of a Business Plan

I.   Description of Business and Ownership
     A) Legal structure
        (sole proprietor, partnership)
        For corporations (C-Corp, S-Corp):
        1. Principal holders' names and addresses
            a) Business affiliations
                (stock and equity ownership)
            b) Degree to which they are involved
                in the business
        2. Business directors' names and addresses
            a) Expertise
            b) Role of board
     B) Amount of stock authorized and issued
     C) State licensing requirement, zoning, insur-
        ance, licenses, and building codes
     D) Trademarks, patents and copyrights

II. Product or Service
     A) Type of business
        (manufacturing, service, construction,
        retail)
     B) Goals and objectives
        1. Description of product or service
        2. Target market
            a) Where to find them
            b) Who buys your product or service
                (1) International, government,
                    commercial, industrial, con-
                    sumer
                (2) Description of consumer
            c) Service or product evaluation
                (1) Market analysis: how is it used?
                    (i)   Performance
                    (ii) Importance of each product
                          or service
                    (iii) Sales projections

        (2)   Marketing strategy: how is it sold?
- (i)   Walk in
- (ii)   Wholesale
- (iii)   Mail (coupon book, flyers, etc.)
- (iv)   Delivery
- (v)   Phone
- (vi)   Advertising (TV., radio, publications, yellow pages)
- (vii) Sales people
- (viii) Trade shows

        (3) Quality and price

        (4) Comparison to competitors' products (services)
- (i)   Advantages
- (ii)   Uniqueness
- (iii)   Disadvantages

        (5) Demand vs. supply

        (6) Customer requirements

        (7) Buying habits and impact on use of your product (service)

C) Location
1. Access of location (freeways, major roads, walking distance, parking)
2. Convenience
3. Easy to find
4. Hours
5. Square footage size needed

III.   Plan of Operation

A) Hiring status
1. Qualifications, skills, traits and abilities
2. Expertise of management and employees
   a) Organizational chart
   b) Key individuals and employees
   c) Résumés and responsibilities
   d) Salaries

B) Contracting outside services

1. Who, what, where, when, how, and why
2. Conditions and duration of contracts

III.   Financial
    A) Accountant, banker, lawyer (name and address)
    B) Controls, cost system and budgets used
        1. Cash basis or accrual
            (a) Cash requirements: now and future years
            (b) Yearly balance sheet, monthly income statement, debt schedule, net worth
            (c) Accounts receivable and payable and aging for the accrual system
    C) Financing
    D) Plans for recession and expansion

Business Plan Exercise Form

1. Description of business and ownership.

2. Goals and objectives of product (service).

3. Plan of operation.

4. Sales strategy (target market, market analysis, and market strategy).

5. Financial.

What Makes Your
Product (Service) Unique?

What (Who) are your main competitors?

List how your competitors' products (services) differ from yours.

Make a list of the ways your products (services) are better or unique and the benefits to your client.

What could you do to take advantage of your company and your strengths to offset your competitors' strengths in a competitive situation?

Mission Statement

The mission statement gives a clear focus on what a business is all about. It specifies what product or service you are offering and your goals and objectives of the organization. It also reflects your credibility, expertise, values, and philosophy of operation.

Criteria for Evaluating Your Mission Statement

- Make sure it is clear and understandable to all involved.

- Make it brief enough for most people to keep it in mind.

- Make sure it specifies what business the organization is in:

  > Specify how it will meet the customer's (client's) needs.

  > Focus on your target market.

  > Specify the product(s)/service(s) that you are offering.

- Make sure it is focused on your goals and objectives of the organization.

- Make sure it reflects your credibility and expertise.

- Make sure it is flexible when it comes to implementation.

- Make sure it can be used as a means to help the organization make decisions.

- Make sure it reflects the organization's values, beliefs, culture, and philosophy of operation.

- Make sure it reflects attainable goals.

Mission Statement Exercise

Facts:

What/Who is your target market?

What are the unique qualities, skills, abilities, and talents you and your company offer?

Emotions:

Using as many of the 5 senses as you can (smell, taste, touch, hearing, vision), list the positive feelings your prospects would get as a result of using your product or service.

What are the emotional benefits your prospects would receive as a result of using your product or service?

My Mission Statement

Setting Goals and Achieving Results

The majority of the population have no goals in life. They just go with the flow hoping that fate or luck will bring them their success. Unfortunately, life doesn't operate that way.

In order to achieve results, you must know specifically what you want. You then need to write a realistic plan for the steps to take for you to achieve your goals.

Finally, pace yourself as you take action to allow for challenges to teach you lessons. Give yourself time for fruition of your plan. Remember, talk is cheap. Actions speak louder than words. In other words, "walk your talk."

Helpful Hints for Achieving Results

1) Always use **Present Tense** — as if it already is occurring (avoid future tripping.)

2) Be **Specific** — a detail description of what it is that you want (not too specific).

3) Use a **Positive Attitude** in wording — not words like: maybe, if, etc.

4) Use **I** or **Me**.

5)   By focusing on **Positive Results**:

   a) Emphasis is on what you want.

   b) You gravitate toward the processes that are most helpful.

   c) You attract those who will be able to help you.

6)   By focusing on **Negative Results**:

   a) Emphasis is on what you don't want.

   b) Get more problems

   c) Results are: conflict, frustrations, fears, etc.

   d) Leading to procrastination, avoidance, and quitting.

   e) Feeling out of control and powerless.

Focusing On
the Main Area

In the space below, list the major goal that you truly want to accomplish, the benefits you'll receive when it's accomplished, and the date and year you want it.

Helpful Hints:

- Be specific: Use "I" or "Me"

- Focus on positive results: Keep your wording positive.

- Write in the present tense as if you have already achieved your major goal.

- Be honest and realistic with the major goal you're working on.

Mind Mapping

Mind Mapping is a creative way to help you achieve your major goal and its rewards. By using the Mind Mapping process, you are allowing what I call the "emotional/feeling" side as well as the "logical/thinking" side to open up.

As you open up to your emotional/feeling side, you will start to create steps that will help you have fun as you work toward achieving your major goal. It is important to understand what benefits these goals will give you because they will help you stay committed to working towards achieving your major goal.

These rewards are emotional gains, material rewards, spiritual attainment, and physical achievements. As you complete your Mind Mapping exercise on the following pages, please remember to have fun and not allow your logical side to take control forcing you to be too specific, rigid, etc.

Mind Mapping Exercise

Tree Trunk (Major Goal)

Branches (Other Goals)
Question each answer with another question in
order to get more specific goal identification.

Flowers (Benefits received for each Goal you accomplish)

Bees (Obstacles/Fears for each Goal)

Honey (Rewards for the Major Goal)

Goals and
Achieving Results

After you do the Mind Mapping Exercise, you can utilize your logical side to list the specific steps you want to take to achieve your goals. You want to do this by prioritizing the steps in order of importance: Emergencies, personal importances, deadlines, long-term tasks and short-term tasks. After you decide these steps, then you start your Plan of Action and Networking.

Here you list your plan and the date you want to accomplish it so you are motivated to take the necessary steps to reach your accomplishments toward your major goal. Setting up meetings with experienced people gives you more insights on various points for which you may not have the answers yourself. These people you want to meet have more knowledge and experience and can guide you with direction on the areas you are striving to accomplish. They can also give you answers to questions you've been struggling to answer. These people can furnish you with information that will clear up your confusion and help you to achieve your end result more efficiently and with more enjoyment.

As you work toward achieving your goals that lead you toward your major goal, you will come across obstacles and fears. They could delay the fruition of your major goal if you procrastinate on taking action to resolve the fears and obstacles.

Learning to solve your challenges and releasing your fears is difficult if you are unaware of them and blame others for them. Usually, when you are unaware and blame others for your challenges and hang-ups, you become angry and anxious, frantically trying to figure out what all this confusion and overwhelming feelings are about. By listing your challenges, you actually see the challenges and help put them in perspective. Your concerns and confusions are re-placed by clarity. You get more insight regarding your common fears.

The most common fears are fear of the un-known, fear of rejection and fear of failing. Learning to recognize these angry and anxious feelings and thoughts is the first step in resolving them. Stay focused and in the present, acknowledging your fears by feeling them, understanding them, and releasing as you acquire wisdom. In "The 3 Most Common Fears" section, which follows, are helpful steps to overcome these popular fears.

The 3 Most Common Fears
(and How to Overcome Them)

Fear of Failing.

- Take it one step at a time (the process) to accomplish the end result.

- Allow for <u>mistakes</u>; they are learning lessons, not <u>failures</u>.

- Acknowledge daily accomplishments.

- Forgive yourself when you miss time deadlines.

- Question and observe people who are already successful in your area.

- Use visualization to help increase positive results.

- Be realistic.

Fear of the Unknown.

- Talk to others who are supportive, positive and trustworthy.

- Pick the brains of educated people who are already successful in your field of learning.

- Stay positive, focused and patient.

- Take things one day at a time.

- Have trust in yourself and God that everything will be taken care of when most needed.

Fear of Rejection.

- Question the area of "concern/rejection" with the individual.

- Look at the worst thing that could happen if rejection occurred.

- Say affirmations (positive words put in present tense in the area in which you're insecure).

- Make things into a joke rather than taking them too seriously.

- Look at rejection as a "not interested" in a particular "thing" rather than personalizing it.

Opportunities of Wisdom

Write about an incident that pushed you out of your comfort zone. Share the obstacles you faced, how you overcame them, and the benefits you achieved as a result of this incident.

List below areas for improvement and steps to take to improve on them:

Tasks to Do to
Accomplish Goals

Start Date: _____

Completed: _____

List Goals below and Prioritize by numbers:

      1   Emergencies

      2   Personal Importances

      3   Deadline (Urgencies/Time)

      4   Short Term or Easy

      5   Long Term or Difficult

_____

_____

_____

_____

_____

_____

_____

_____

_____

_____

_____

_____

_____

_____

Notes Page

Time Management
and Organizational Skills

Effective time management is organizing your time so that you utilize it in the most productive way as you eliminate your time wasters.

Some of these time wasters are negative people, worrying about a particular area in your life, working harder versus working smarter, putting too much time into things you don't understand or have the answers to, ineffective organizational skills, and other similar obstacles.

All of these time wasters take valuable time out of your otherwise productive schedules. By learning what your time wasters are, you are able to eliminate them, be more efficient, and have more time on your hands to enjoy life by living a balanced life.

Time Wasters

Overly high standards

•

Assuming others' responsibilities

•

The desire to please others.

•

Lack of organization.

•

Constant interruptions.

•

Lots of trivial activities.

•

Procrastination.

•

Fears: failing, rejection, unknown

On what items are you spending too much time?

How is it affecting you and other parts of your life?

What steps can you take to resolve these time wasters?

Winning the Race Against Time

The following are some ways that you can save yourself valuable time. Read them over and try to identify the areas where you are wasting time.

1. Set personal goals and objectives.

2. When faced with an overwhelming job, break it down into more easily managed tasks.

3. Determine your most productive time of the day, either morning, afternoon, or evening. Do your important tasks then.

4. Do your unpleasant tasks as soon as possible in order to get them out of the way.

5. Arrange for some uninterrupted time each day.

6. Don't get bogged down in menial tasks.

7. Avoid people who are time wasters and have a negative focus.

8. Mark appointments immediately on your calendar.

9. Write reminders to yourself.

10. Keep a list of concerns. It helps to minimize their importance.

11. Keep a time log to see how much time is spent on tasks. You will start to see a pattern of time wasters.

12. Learn not to take care of other peoples' challenges and tasks.

13. Set time limits for meetings.

14. Learn to recognize your limits and say no to people.

15. Take time for personal recreation and family activities (balanced living).

16. Return phone calls in bunches.

17. Be flexible and open minded to others' suggestions. They could benefit you in time consumption and in avoiding unnecessary frustrations.

18. Be direct and specific regarding what you want.

19. Delegate, when necessary, to the people who are most qualified.

20. Work ahead of schedule when possible.

Plan of Action

For each of the previous Tasks to Accomplish, list below your plan of action.

Plan of Action/Date Started/Target Date to Complete:

Plan of Action/Date Started/Target Date to Complete:

Plan of Action/Date Started/Target Date to Complete:

Plan of Action/Date Started/Target Date to Complete:

Plan of Action/Date Started/Target Date to Complete:

Plan of Action/Date Started/Target Date to Complete:

Plan of Action/Date Started/Target Date to Complete:

Plan of Action/Date Started/Target Date to Complete:

Plan of Action/Date Started/Target Date to Complete:

Plan of Action/Date Started/Target Date to Complete:

Plan of Action/Date Started/Target Date to Complete

Plan of Action/Date Started/Target Date to Complete:

Networking Plans
(People to talk to, locations, etc.)

People and Comments:

People and Comments:

People and Comments:

People and Comments:

People and Comments:

People and Comments:

Effective Decision Making

After dealing with your emotional confusion, frustrations, fears, and anger, you want to sit down and say, "What steps can I take to resolve this?" Begin by listing them and then take the necessary steps to resolve those challenges.

As you take responsibility for your actions and results, you will create the fruitions you deserve. Use strategy to resolve the obstacles by taking responsibility for your actions and the results of them. The way to take responsibility for your actions is to collect all the facts on the challenge you are presently facing. You may not presently have all the facts, which I call pieces of the puzzle, to help you solve the challenge.

Patience, persistence, time, and faith will bring you the missing pieces so that you have clarity and understanding. When you get all the necessary facts, you will be able to come up with solutions, choosing the best solution with justified reasons for that solution.

Finally, have the confidence and courage, and take the proper action for that solution, and allow yourself to make mistakes as you learn and grow from them. If you have doubts on what decision to make, it could be because you have gotten too emotionally involved, causing confusion. You may be unsure as to whether to leave the situation as it is or to change it. I have put together a formula to help you resolve this confusion. I call this the "Decision Making Formula" (see page 48: "Solving Your Challenges Worksheet"). In this formula, you are listing all the reasons for changing to the reasons for keeping it as it is. Then you decide which weighs more in importance to your well being and happiness. That answer will give you the direction for which way to go.

Sometimes people get too involved in the process of getting their major goal, plugging away from one thing to the next. They beat themselves up with judgments and criticism when they are not doing what they want or accomplishing their major goal sooner.

When these people do accomplish their goals, they sometimes don't take the time to enjoy the fruition because they are so tired from pushing themselves to get this fruition.

Periodically reviewing and summarizing what you have done gives you your opportunities of wisdom. In your opportunities of wisdom, you are seeing how you pushed yourself out of your comfort zone in many areas, giving you the confidence and motivation to keep plugging along to the next step. Hopefully, you reward yourself internally with personal satisfaction and externally with gifts.

On the following pages are steps on solving your challenges, ideas to overcome stress, and ways to get out of feeling guilty and resentful.

Solving Your Challenges Worksheet

1. List a personal challenge or situation that you want to resolve.

2. Why do you want to work on this area? Use the formula below to help you see the benefits of working on this area.

Decision Making Formula

Reasons for Changing:

Reasons for Staying As Is:

3. Using the formula below, list the steps to help you with your challenge.

Examine the Challenge

List what you know about the situation.

List **all** the solutions: Research and Advice from Knowledgeable People.

Pick a solution and write about it.

Justify with reasons and with conviction.

List Your Challenges

Challenges:

Challenges:

Challenges:

Challenges:

Challenges:

Challenges:

Steps to Resolving Concerns

Steps to resolve concerns:

Steps to resolve concerns:

Steps to resolve concerns:

Steps to resolve concerns:

Steps to resolve concerns:

Ways Out of Guilt and Resentment

1. **Change the Image:**

   - Ask yourself, "What am I upset about?"

   - Be honest and realistic with the response.

   - Accept the response.

   - Give yourself and others permission to make their mistakes. You don't have to like it, but you don't have to hate it either.

2. **Forgive:**

   - For judging yourself and others.

   - For the action or situation that occurred.

   - And remember, good people do not always do good things. That makes them human.

3. **What's the Payoff?**

   - Are you enjoying the intensity?

   - What are you getting from this?

4. **Exercise.**

   - Do physical exercise.

   - Keep energy moving by not oversleeping or procrastinating.

5. **Focus.**

   - Focus on the positive.

   - Accept what you consider to be negative — they are opportunities for growth. Be grateful for them because they help you to establish more wisdom.

6. **Show Gratitude.**

   - Be thankful for what you have, and what you **don't** have.

7. **Observe.**

   - Allow yourself to feel the feelings.

   - Observing helps you to understand and learn from the situation.

8. **Breathe.**

   - For meditators: Breathe with a white light going in with each breath and filling your body.

   - Non-meditators: Breathe in deeply so that you feel it in your stomach. Then, hold it for 4 seconds.

9. **Surrender.**

   - Let go of the internal struggle.

   - Do not try to rid the feelings. Allow them, and heal them with comfort.

Fear turns into guilt or resentment.

Guilt and resentment turn into anger.

Anger turns into negativity.

Summary on Solving Your Challenges

Denial — Blame   Trigger: Anger or Anxiousness

               ↗   Procrastinate

Fear → Quit

               ↘   Go On

Awareness (emotions involved here) is 95% of solving the problem.

               ↗   Procrastinate

Fear → Quit

               ↘   Go On

Stages (constructive problem solving):

- Get all the facts.
- Get all the solutions.
- Pick the best solution with a justified reason for that selection.

               ↗   Procrastinate

Fear → Quit

               ↘   Go On

Practice (mistakes occur here)

               ↗   Procrastinate

Fear → Quit

               ↘   Go On

Skill achieved — success accomplished.

Start with a new challenge!

Major Factors to Observe
and Learn From

1. List the desired goal, for the time period you are reviewing, in specific detail.

2. List the major factors that stand out in striving for your goal (people, companies, other obstacles).

3. List your achievements and the lessons you learned as a result of each major factor.

Summary:

1. Review previous questions 1, 2, and 3, and summarize with a list of common areas.

2. What are the gains?

3. What were the lessons you learned as a result of the common obstacles or challenges?

Increasing Your Client Base

In this chapter I will be discussing ways in which you can increase your client base. It is important to plan how and where to get your clients so that you can achieve a steady increase in your client base. This will be more fun than frantically and desperately grabbing anyone or anything that comes your way. No one needs to be on an emotional roller coaster, experiencing hills and valleys in their profits.

As you read this chapter and learn various ways to achieve more business, you may want to try some of the suggestions that you've never tried before, especially the ones that seem uncomfortable for you.

Measuring your results is important since it will help you to make sure you're spending your time and dollars in the most productive areas. It also helps to improve on the necessary personal and professional skill development areas for more confidence and satisfaction.

Monthly Sales Projections

Setting monthly sales projections and actuals are important — just as important as setting and achieving your major goals in life. By setting your sales projections, you will be able to plan how to improve your sales volume. It helps you to measure your process of where and how you get your sales, and look for areas that need improvement.

In the exercise that follows, please fill out your sales plan. After observing your process for a period of time, you'll want to notice how you have improved or what areas need improving.

Monthly Sales Projections and Actuals Exercise

Plan of operation (how and where you will get your sales).

Sales Projections to Actuals

Projected Sales   _____

Actual Sales   _____

Percentage Change (-)_____

Reason for Change

What improved?

What could be improved?

Pre-Planning

Prospects buy from people they trust. The process of building trust is through relationship building. The more you understand the traits and behavioral styles of the prospects you are targeting, the easier it will be to build a relationship.

Pre-planning is an effective way to help you learn about the prospect and their industry prior to meeting them. As you do your pre-planning, you will be educating yourself regarding industry trends, growth patterns, history, and market share. This will serve to enhance your confidence in relationship selling.

You will also learn more about the decision makers' special hobbies, interests and their challenges. Being genuinely interested in the decision makers' business needs and finding ways to meet them with your product (service) can be used to turn them from prospect to client. Giving honest and sincere compliments and respecting the decision maker as a person are excellent ways to build initial trust and rapport.

It's important to learn who the decision makers are and what they're doing for two reasons. One, to acquire knowledge needed for building relationships with your current prospects. And, second, to acquire additional business. Pre-planning will give you the tools to know how to develop stronger business relationships which can result in more business and referrals. The steps in doing pre-planning are as follows:

1. Choose a company or industry you want as a client.

2. Use the following sources to research the company or industry:

Library.
Secretary.
Clients within the same company or industry.
Annual Report.
Contacts Influential book.

3. Learn about the competitors' growth, history, trends, market share, etc.

Where to Get Business: Networking and Resources

Networking is one of the most effective ways to get business because you develop solid business relationship and referrals. There are many places you can network. Listed below are the suggested places to network:

Chamber of Commerce:

They have lead groups to swap business cards.

They have networking breakfasts.

They have happy hours.

They have educational seminars.

Social Events:

You can meet lots of people and acquire leads in a comfortable setting.

Health Club:

If you go to a club during set times, you will eventually see the regulars where you can develop a relationship.

Other Resources:

Personal Life: Your doctors, lawyers, insurance agent.

Influential Contacts.

Yellow Pages

New business listings.

Marketing Letters

Marketing letters are used to introduce your product or service to new prospects and to introduce additional products or services to your existing customers. When you write marketing letters, you want to get a clear picture of whom your audience is, what their interests, skills and passions are, and their socio-economic or educational level.

Ways to Write a Business Letter

1. Picture your audience when you write:

   What are their interests, skills and passions?

   What is their socio-economic or educational level?

   What do they need to know?

2. Be clear, informal, and personal.

3. Begin with your main point and lead to a conclusion or recommendation by way of support data.

   Example: "Because orders have increased by 50% in the past 6 months, I recommend that we hire 2 additional staff people."

4. Don't use too much passive voice. (Passive voice is when the person doing the action isn't in the sentence or is hiding behind the preposition "by.")

   Example: "It has been determined that..." (Passive)

   "My partner and I have determined..." (Non-passive)

5. Be specific, not general, in order to make it stick in the reader's mind.

 Example: "The quality guidelines used for manu-facturing cars are declining. (General)

    "Since 1960, cars are made using cheaper parts." (Specific)

How to Write a Sales Letter

1. Make the purpose of the letter clear in the first paragraph.

2. Don't attempt to be funny or clever.

3. Avoid slang or trite expressions.

4. Be personal (yourself).

5. Be aware of the quirks, the likes, and dislikes of your customer or prospect.

6. Ask for action.

7. Make the letter long enough to accomplish the desired objective.

8. Be concise and effective in order to hold the reader's interest.

Sales Letters

Example 1

Prospect's competitors doing business with you:

"As a (title of person) who is undoubtedly interested in increasing your company's effectiveness and productivity, you are probably interested in knowing what your competitors are doing to accomplish ex-actly that. With this goal in mind, I will contact you (specific date and time). Please accept my call."

Example 2

Same company doing business with you in other locations:

"Your company and mine have been doing business together for some time. Just last month our companies did business together in (location, location, location)." I will be contacting you (specific date and time) to set an appointment and to show you how we can help you (list a benefit they will receive that will make them want to meet with you.) Please accept my call."

Example 3

Prospect's company — other locations and their competitor:

"As a (title of person) who is undoubtedly interested in increasing your company's effectiveness and productivity, you are probably interested in knowing what your own company and your competitors are doing in other locations to accomplish exactly that. With this goal in mind, I will contact you (specific date and time). Please accept my call."

People Letter
(sample)

Date

Name/Address

Dear: (Name of person)

Executive decisions are carried out by PEOPLE.

By far, the largest single item in any operating budget is PEOPLE.

Most planning centers around the needs and abilities of PEOPLE.

The biggest and most valuable asset any company has is its PEOPLE.

By actual measurement, the average executive spends three-quarters of each working day dealing with PEOPLE.

Jeanette L. Rosenberg, the owner of Advance Success Unlimited, has earned a unique place in the business sector. People of all ethnic backgrounds and occupations learn the techniques and language to help them do their job. Yet, they may be unable to communicate their knowledge and work effectively with others. This could lead to high stress, low self esteem and low productivity.

Achieving success is accomplished when you can utilize your knowledge to achieve effective outcomes and to have the ability to get along with others in the process. Jeanette L. Rosenberg helps others to develop these skills in their everyday life.

Isn't your company worth it? I will be contacting you within the next few days to set up an appointment so that we can discuss what I can do for you and your company.

Sincerely,

Jeanette L. Rosenberg

Cold Calling

There is a difference between cold calls and warm calls. Cold calls are defined here as door-to-door where you are meeting someone for the first time. Warm calls are calls to people you have already met.

There are advantages and disadvantages to cold calling. The advantages are that you are able to do a brief introduction on what your product (service) is all about. Depending on what product (service) you are offering, this could be a very profitable way to drum up new business.

The disadvantages of using cold calling as a means of getting new business are that they are time consuming, and the initial costs can outweigh the profits. Think about the driving time you spend to do the cold calling, the gas, costs for the materials you may leave, and the actual time that you spend doing the cold calling. This time takes away from other things that you could be doing. The best way to see if cold calling is a profitable way to get business is to measure your return on your investment.

Calculating your worth per hour is a starting point in figuring out what your investment is compared to what you receive in sales income. When you are figuring out if cold calling is a profitable way to get more business, you use your non-selling worth per hour and compare it with the cost accumulated doing the cold calling. If the cold calling expense (driving time, fuel, time spent cold calling, and materials cost) outweighs the return in profits, then cold calling may not be your best approach in getting business. Figure your worth per hour using the following formula in "Calculating Your Worth.".

Calculating Your Worth

Selling

1. Formula for figuring your worth per hour in selling:

$$\frac{\text{(Net \$ earned in the time period)}}{\text{(Total hours worked in the time period)}}$$

2. Formula for calculating the percent of time spent selling:

$$\frac{\text{(time spent selling in the time period}}{\text{(total hours worked in the time period)}}$$

3. Formula for figuring worth per hour in non-selling:

(Net $ per hour) X (the % of time spent selling)
equals (worth per hour in selling)

Non-Selling

1. Formula for calculating the percent of time spent non-selling:

$$\frac{\text{(net \$ earned in the time period)}}{\text{(the total hours worked in the time period)}}$$

2. Formula for calculating the percent of time spent non-selling:

$$\frac{\text{(time spent non-selling in the time period)}}{\text{(total hours worked in the time period)}}$$

3. Formula for worth per hour in non-selling:

(net $ per hour) X (the % of time spent non-selling) = (worth per hour in non-selling)

Example A: Calculate the worth per hour per week for both selling and non-selling.

Selling

40 hours/week made $1000 in that week:
$1000/40 hours = $25 per hour

<u>10 selling hours</u>
40 total hours
equals
25% of time is spent selling
$25 per hour x 25% = $6.25 per hour in selling

$6.25 equals your worth per hour in selling

Non-selling

40/hours/week made $1000 in that week:
$1000/40 hours = $25 per hour

<u>30 non-selling hours</u>
40 hours
equals
75% of time is spent non-selling
$25 per hour x 75%= $18.75 per hour in non-selling

$18.75 equals your worth per hour non-selling

Example B: Keeping the worth per hour per week and the closing ratio the same as in Example A, but increasing the selling hours and decreasing the non-selling hours:

Selling

<u>18 hours selling</u>
40 hour week
equals
45% of time is spent in selling
$25 per hour x 45% = $11.25 per hour in selling

$11.25 equals your worth selling versus $6.25 in Example A, or an 80% increase in your selling hourly worth!

Non-Selling

$$\frac{22 \text{ hours non-selling}}{40 \text{ hour week}}$$

equals

55% of time is spent non-selling

$25 per hour x 55% = $13.75 per hour non-selling

$13.75 equals your worth non-selling versus $18.75 spent selling

Note:

Even though you are worth $5 more per hour selling ($11.25-$6.25=$5), you had to work 8 hours more to make the same $1000 commission. Why do you have to work harder to make a sale?

Possible areas to improve:

- sales skills

- communication and listening skills

- relationship building

- customer satisfaction

Please list below your current worth per hour and today's date.

Current worth per hour_____

Date today_____

Tips on Cold Calling

Cold calling is defined here as door to door.

> A cold call is someone you've never met.
>
> A warm call is someone you've already met.

Determine if this is the best way to get business.

> Using your non-selling worth per hour, weigh and see how much business you receive compared to the time and cost accumulated doing the cold calling.

If cold calling expense (driving time, fuel, time spent cold calling) outweighs the return in profits, then it may not be your best approach in getting business.

Rejection Formula:

> Figure out the number of No's you get before you get a Yes.

What to say when you call for an appointment:

> Get an appointment (versus selling) on the phone.
>
> Try not to give the price on the phone (to avoid being rejected based on price alone).
>
> Make sure it is a good time to talk before continuing on to get the appointment.
>
> Tell them the purpose of your call, stating how the prospect would benefit by meeting with you.
>
> **Example:**
>
> "Is this a good time to call? I left material (my card) with (person's name) on (day). The purpose of my call is to set an appointment with you to discuss (benefits your product/

service can do for them). Would morning or afternoon be better for you?"

Best time to cold call:

Prior to appointments you have in the same area.

Early in the morning.

During lunch hours when the original secretary is out.

Friday afternoons because it is more easy going.

How to cold call:

Drop off your business card (materials) with the secretary or person in charge.

Build an ally with the secretary or person in charge.

Get the owner's name (decision maker) and do "pre-planning" on the company.

Find out what the best times are to call.

Make sure that the company is qualified to buy your product (service).

Telemarketing

Another way to get more business is through telemarketing. You can get appointments and/or sales on the telephone, depending on what type of selling you are doing. In this section, I will be discussing how to get appointments on the telephone. This includes giving lots of information about what your product (service) does and the price.

If you give the prospects too much information prior to seeing them, they may make a premature decision to not see you. You want to make sure it is a good time to talk before continuing on to get the appointment. Then, you want to tell them the purpose of the call, stating how they would benefit by meeting with you. For example, "Is this a good time to call? The purpose of my call is to set an appointment with you to discuss (benefits of what your product / service can do for them). Would morning or afternoon be better for you?"

If you dropped off information prior to your call, you can use this example as an opening: "Is this a good time to call? I left material (my card, brochure) with (person's name) on (day). The purpose of my call is to set an appointment with you to discuss (benefits of what your product /service can do for them). Would morning or afternoon be better for you?"

Telemarketing Notes

Telemarketing is defined here as getting appointments and/or sales on the telephone.

> 38% of salespeople make 1 call and give up.
>
> 23% of sales people make 2 calls and give up.
>
> 19% of salespeople make 3 calls and give up.
>
> 20% of sales people make 4 or more calls and don't give up

Note: Prospects may be qualified and answered rudely due to having a bad day or being uninformed about what you have or do.

Buyer Thoughts:

- Who is calling?
- Do I want to be interrupted?
- What do you want?
- Why should I listen to you?
- What is in it for me?

Salesperson's Approach:

- Introduce by name and company.
- Ask if it is a good time to call.
- Give the purpose of the call.
- Tell what it is you're selling.
- Tell the prospect the benefits of meeting with you (something common to industry that is needed).

Examples:

How you can:

- Save money.
- Make money.
- Improve quality.
- Increase profit.
- Improve customer service.

Phone Script

Mr./Mrs. (name),

I understand you are the (title of company).

Is my information correct?

Mr./Mrs. (prospect),

As a/the (title),

You are probably always looking for ways to (initial reasons for buying).

Would I still be correct?

My purpose in calling is to determine a time when I can stop by and bring you up to date on what other (companies, competitors, industry names) are doing to improve (initial reasons for buying).

Would (time or time) be better for you?

Example of Setting Appointments on the Telephone

Prospect

I'd like to get some information on your product (service).

Salesperson

Fine. Were you calling for yourself?

Prospect

Yes.

Salesperson

How did you hear about us?

Prospect

From your ad in the paper.

Salesperson

What are you hoping to achieve from (your product or service)?

Prospect

The prospect tells you their initial reason(s) for buying.

Salesperson

Why is this important to you?

Prospect

The prospect tells you their concerns, fears, etc.

Salesperson

You're probably wondering how we do this, what some of the costs may be, the time frame, etc. Is this correct? (Optional)

Prospect

Yes.

Salesperson

We find that the best way to answer these and other questions which may arise is to sit down, learn more about your needs, and educate you on how we can help. This usually This usually takes 20-25 minutes and by that time or before, we'll both know if (product/ service) has what you're looking for. If we do, we can pursue it further. Does that sound reasonable?

Prospect

Yes.

Salesperson

Who else would be involved in helping you with your decision making?

Prospect

My husband (wife).

Salesperson

Let's invite him (her) so we can answer any questions.

Prospect

Fine.

Salesperson

Is morning or afternoon better for both of you?

Prospect

Morning.

Salesperson

I have (time) or (time) open.

Prospect

(Time).

Salesperson

My name is Juliett. I look forward to meeting you both.

Monthly Telemarketing and Measurement Plan

1.   What did you do right in your telemarketing?

2.   What areas can you improve in?

Ratios

Calls to appointment _____

Appointment to sales _____

% Increase in appts. compared to last month _____

% Increase in sales compared to last month _____

5

Steps For Increasing Sales Volume

In this section, I will be discussing various tools to help you increase your sales volume. You will learn how to weed out the unqualified potential clients (customers) and pre-plan for sales appointments.

You will also learn how to relate better with others through effective communications and listening skills, understand how others process information, and put together an effective presentation.

Weeding Out the Non-Prospect

It is tempting for the sales representative to make call-back after call-back in the hope that the lukewarm buyer can be made into a hot prospect. Further, it is a common error in selling to call again and again on the wrong person — one who hasn't the authority to buy. You may be asking at this point, "how do you detect a non-prospect?" Listed below are some guidelines to help you detect a non-prospect.

How to Detect a Non-Prospect

1. Stay focused during your presentation.

2. Listen to what is being said, not what you want to hear.

3. Listen to your gut feeling as to whether the prospect is qualified or unqualified.

4. Watch the way the prospect behaves:

    - Is the prospect's body language showing positive or negative interest?

    - Does the prospect have good eye contact?

    - Is the prospect asking questions about your service or product?

    - Is the prospect offering comments that would help him/her utilize your service or product?

    - Do you have the prospect's undivided attention?

- Is the prospect doing too much "head nodding," showing politeness more than interest?

5. Are you talking with the decision maker? The decision maker can be the person with rank and authority. Many top executives delegate purchasing decisions to low-ranking employees. Ask , "are there others involved in this proposition or are you the one to make the decision?"

6. After the presentation, analyze your presentation and sales approach for improvement and growth.

Your Credibility and Company Credentials

In this section you will be learning how to establish credibility and build rapport with your prospects as you build a business relationship with them. According to *Success* magazine, **it takes 7 seconds to gain attention.** Handshakes are one way to understand what type of person the prospect is and a way for the prospect to understand you as well. Handshakes can give information like whether someone is warm and friendly or controlling. There are 4 types of handshakes listed below. Observe their handshakes to see if they are:

- Jellyfish: Limp hand. Gives the impression of being insecure.

- Knuckle Breaker: Your hands are gripped. This is the power play of a controlling person.

- Finger Squeezer: Grabs your fingers with a light touch. Gives the impression of being prissy and unsure as to whether he/she wants to touch your whole hand.

- Covered Handshake: Left hand over the hands clasped in the handshake. Perceived as a warm and caring person. The other person may feel that they're being patronized.

After the handshake, you want to make a good impression in the way you present yourself. Giving honest and sincere compliments can help to break the ice and develop rapport. It is to your advantage to learn what you can about the person as a whole.

What type of personality are they and what style do they use to process the information that they are hearing? There are 4 types of personalities:

- Quick and to the point
- Laid back/Melancholic
- Analytical/Observant
- Personable/Outgoing

The personality type that is "quick and to the point" wants information given quickly and concisely. They are impatient and get bored easily with long, drawn-out conversations.

The "laid back/melancholic" type thrives on long, drawn-out conversations. They are relaxed and slow in processing things and come across as incompetent to the "quick and to the point" personality type.

The "analytical/observant" type likes lots of information to dissect. They need plenty of facts, benefits, and space to analyze on their own time.

The "personable/outgoing" type is talkative and friendly. They can come across as a party person, one who likes to play more than work. You normally find these people in sales since they love to be around lots of people.

The more you understand personality types — yours and your prospect — the easier it becomes to build trust and rapport with them.

Credibility

It is necessary to establish credibility because it shows your prospects that you are experienced and knowledgeable about the product or service you are selling.

Start by asking permission to educate them on the overview of both your company and your uniqueness. This is an important step because you are sharing how knowledgeable you are about your business and what makes you unique — your talents, skills, and abilities — which helps to develop confidence in the prospect.

Here is an example of what you can say before you educate them about your company and your uniqueness: "Now that I've learned a little bit about you, do you mind if I tell you a little bit about me and my company?"

Communication

Communication is a wonderful way to express yourself, and yet it's so complex! It's not only what you say but how you say it. There are various levels of communication you go through when you meet someone and build a business relationship. When you first meet someone, you talk "small talk" which is unspecific and brief. As you build a relationship with them, you ask more questions, share opinions, and reveal more feelings. Listed next are the levels of communication you go through as you get to know the other person.

Levels of Communication

Getting to know the other person:

- Small talk
- Open-ended questioning
- Sharing an opinion
- Revealing feelings more

Relationship building:

- Sharing feelings about yourself and things about the other person
- Discussing differences
- Tuned in with the other person, total understanding

Keys to Understanding Conversation:

There is also the way in which you communicate. Communication is broken down into three components: Content, body language, and context.

Depending on what percentage one uses in each of these components during communication will affect how well the listener hears, understands and remembers.

Studies were done on how your brain picks up information and remembers it. They found that the most effective way to communicate, using each of the above components, is through "body language" (55%). "Content" accounts for 7% and "context" was 38%. Again, it's not only what you say, but how you say it.

Content 7%

Body Language 55%

Context (Voice, Tone, Words) 38%

Attitude is also important when communicating. If you are having a lousy day, your tone of voice, pitch, pace of speaking, and body language may show it. If you are in a bad mood, your tone of voice can show anger, frustration, etc.

Your tone of voice states your emotions and whether or not you have a positive or negative attitude. Your pitch and the pace in which you speak is also a tool used to express your attitude. A variety is more interesting and will draw people toward you. If the pitch is too high or too low, it will sound strained and irritate the listener. If your pace is too slow, you can bore the listener and lose their attention. If your pace is too fast, it may be difficult to understand, thereby losing the listener's confidence and trust.

Pace of Speaking

Too slow: bores people, lose their attention.

Too fast: difficult to understand, lost the confidence and trust of the listener.

Non-words: Insecure, loses the confidence and trust of the listener. (Words such as "um," "uh-huh," etc.)

Tone

It's not only what you say; it's how you say it. Tone states your emotions and attitude.

Pitch

A variety is more interesting and will draw the listener toward you. If it is too low it will sound strained and irritate the listener.

Rapport Building

Communication styles are the way people process information that they are hearing. They can process it in one of three ways: visual, auditory, or kinesthetic.

Visual is someone who processes by **seeing** the information. Auditory is someone who processes by **hearing** the information. And, a Kinesthetic is someone who processes by **analyzing, relying heavily on their emotions or intuition**.

Depending on the situation, a person can use one or more of these styles in processing. Normally, an individual will dominate in one of these three styles. When you first meet the prospect, they are using the unspecific language or businesslike words and mannerisms. Once you start to earn their trust and build rapport, the prospect will show what type of communication style is most comfortable for them in the present situation.

Listed on the following pages are the communication styles people use as they process information to build relationships.

Communication Styles*

As you communicate and listen to your prospect, observe their body language, posture, words they use, and pace of speech. In this way, you can identify whether they are auditory, kinesthetic, or visual.

Unspecific: Businesslike words and mannerisms. Use of "small talk." What you say is, "how, specifically" to get them to open up:

know	experience
understand	think
process	decide
change	perceive

Visual: High pitch, nasal, talking fast, upper chest breathing, shoulders back, head tilted upward, chin up, eyes looking upward, left to right (sky):

see	picture
reveal	appear
illuminate	envision
imagine	view

Auditory: Melodic talk, diaphragm breathing, shoulders straight, head tilting forward, eyes looking forward, left to right (ears):

hear	listen
sound	say
tune in	discuss
expression	attune

Kinesthetic: Low pitch, slow talk, deep sighing, catching their breath, stomach breathing, shoulders rounded and forward, head tilted down, eyes looking down, left to right (stomach):

down	feel
touch	pressing
aware	hands-on
irritate	grasp

How one perceives their beliefs:

Everyone processes their Belief System differently. The way one processes information or beliefs can be totally opposite from the way another person processes the same information as listed below:

Toward - gaining from a situation
Away - run away from a situation

Self - "I", "Me"
Others - "We", "Them"

Mismatch - fault finder
Match - comparing

External - rely on what others say
Internal - rely on their intuition, trust

Possibility - relying on level of importance of what **could** be
Necessity - relying on guidelines and boundaries based on **feelings**

10 Traits of a Master Salesperson

1. **Persistence**

   There's a lot of difference between **persistence** and **insistence**. Persistence wins respect; insistence annoys. The Master Salesperson hangs on a bit longer, and works a little harder than the average salesperson.

2. **Creativity**

   Talk to Master Salespersons and you will be impressed with how they use their creativity. Notice how they use their creativity for practical plans and overcoming challenges.

3. **Vision**

   For the Master Salespersons, the present is always just the beginning. They are impressed with the possibilities of the future and are excited to make the most of their opportunities.

4. **Integrity**

   The Master Salespersons pride themselves on the fact that their word is good. They don't make promises they can't keep.

5. **Sincerity**

   Master Salespersons are sincere in their interest in the other person and are excited to be of really worthwhile service to that person.

6. **Conviction**

   The successful producers talk to everyone with confidence and ease. They know they're right, so they tell their story with poise and conviction.

7. **Positive Attitude**

   The outstanding salespersons don't dwell on the past. They learn from their mistakes and focus on the future. Constructive thinking deals with the future.

8. **Common Sense**

Common sense is a little more than good judgment at work, based upon reason. It is using your logic and intuition to make sound effective decisions.

9. **Self Confidence**

The Master Salespersons respect themselves and others. They know their values and follow through with them as they speak honestly and persuasively.

10. **Initiative**

Initiative is "try it and see it now." The prospect who is hard to see, the program that is difficult to tackle are each tasks that the Master Salespersons go after with vigor.

Finding Motive to Buy

Questioning is an important step because it gives you the prospect's initial reasons for buying (their wants) and their true emotional reason for buying (their desire). You want to question them until you feel confident that you have their true emotional buying motive. A helpful hint on achieving their emotional buying motive is to question each answer they give to get more and more specific answers for clarity and understanding.

1. **Purpose of Questioning:**
   - Find initial reasons for buying (the prospect's wants).
   - Find emotional reason for buying (true desire).

2. **Question to Find Prospects Needs:**

   Example: "In order to save you time and see if I may be of service to you, do you mind if I ask you some questions?"

   Question each answer with another question in order to further define and clarify.

3. **Two Types of Questions:** (You want to alternate between the two.)
   - Open ended. Lets the prospect talk.
   - Close ended. "Yes" or "No" answers.

4. **3 Areas to Question:**
   - Decision Maker: Find out the name of the decision maker who is involved in the decision making and the history of the decision making.
   - Challenges: Find out their challenges and fears.
   - Benefits/Gains: Find out how they can benefit or gain from doing business with you.

How to Learn More
About Your Prospect

In this exercise, use the following words to start each question that you would ask your prospect: Who, What, Where, When, How, and Why.

Learning About the Individual

Challenges

<u>Benefits and Gains</u>

Formula for Improving
Listening Skills: LOVE

(L)isten

Concentrate without letting your mind wander or jumping in to talk.

Example of good listening: Nodding head in agreement.

Example of poor listening: Constant non-words (uh hum, OK, etc.)

(O)bserve

Observe first with your eyes and then with your ears (body language, tone of voice, expression on the face) without using personal biases.

(V)erify

Repeat what you heard using some of their words. Don't offer advice unless asked.

(E)mpathize

Mentally involved, supportive. Putting yourself in their shoes and observing their situation. Acknowledging their feelings behind their words as you repeat what you heard so the listener feels understood. (Note: This skill is used mostly with challenges.)

Sympathize (ineffective way)

Emotionally involved or commiserating. Feeling responsible for their problems. Trying to "rescue" them or join them in their pain.

Improving Your Communication Skills

1. Make sure you are speaking the same language (semantics)

2. Repeat what you heard to make sure you heard the person correctly.

3. Listen attentively. Don't let the mind wander or do other activities.

4. Wait until the person is finished speaking, instead of interrupting with your thoughts.

5. Don't assume you know what the person is going to say.

6. Define what you want and be specific in the way you say it.

7. Don't criticize, judge, or use bias.

8. Don't argue or become defensive with others' opinions.

9. Be complimentary and empathic.

10. Be open minded and flexible.

11. If the person's comments are unclear, ask questions rather than guess at what they are trying to say.

12. Ask questions or make suggestions instead of telling people what to do.

13. Share their enthusiasm by mirroring their behavior.

14. See through the speaker's eyes when they communicate — to avoid listening with your own biases.

Checklist for Effective
Listening and Communication

<u>Listen</u>

- Did I make sure I was speaking the same language (semantics)?
- Did I listen attentively, not letting my mind wander or do other activities?
- Was I open minded and flexible?
- Did I jump into the middle of the conversation?
- Did I assume I knew what the person was going to say?
- Did I interrupt and finish the sentence with my thoughts?

<u>Observe</u>

- Did I observe the body language as well as the verbal language?
- Was I open minded and flexible?
- Did I share their enthusiasm by mirroring their behavior?
- Did I see through their eyes when they communicated, avoiding my own biases?
- Did I argue or become defensive with others' opinions?

<u>Verify</u>

- Did I repeat what I heard to make sure I heard the person correctly?
- Did I ask questions when the person's comments were unclear instead of guessing what they were trying to say?
- Did I criticize, judge, or use my own biases?
- Did I argue or become defensive with others' opinions?

<u>Empathize</u>

- Was I supportive without commiserating?
- Was I complimentary?
- Did I acknowledge the person's feelings behind their words so the person feels understood?
- Was I compassionate and empathic?
- Was I open minded and flexible?
- When asked for advice, did I do so by asking questions or making suggestions?
- Did I offer advice by telling them what to do?
- Did I criticize, judge or use my own biases?
- Did I argue or become defensive with others' opinions?

Test Closes

Test closes are test closing questions you ask the prospects to make sure that they understand what you are saying. They are a way of finding out if they're interested in what you're selling. Test closes are used throughout the presentation, from the questioning step through closing the sale. They help make sure that you haven't lost the prospects' attention, interest or confused them. Communicate the test closes in a positive format, not negative or demeaning.

Examples: Would you agree?

Sounds good, doesn't it?

What are you feeling?

If you had this product (service), would you find this option useful?

Below is a list of points to keep in mind when doing your test closes:

**Sale: Giving Your Presentation
vs. No Sale: Skepticism**

- Make sure you've heard all the prospect's initial reasons for buying and their true emotional buying motive.

- Present facts, benefits, evidence, and use test closes.

- Make a list of facts and benefits about your company product (service).

- Make a list of test closes.

- Demonstrate showmanship, enthusiasm, a positive attitude and convictions when presenting your product (service).

- Prospects buy from people who believe in themselves and their product (service).

- Be specific and to the point.

- Express yourself using a similar personality type as the prospect to keep the rapport.

- Please turn to "Communication Style" on pages 88-89 so that you can talk their language.

- Don't oversell — self or company.

- Focus on their needs, not yours.

**Sale: More Information
vs. No Sale: Procrastination**

- Turn the prospects' wants to emotional reasons to purchase by:

- Repeating what they lack, and show them how you can solve their lack or what they can gain by using your product (service).

- Using enthusiasm, positive attitudes, and conviction.

- Using showmanship (testimonials, exhibits, references, etc.).

- Use test closes.

Objections are merely questions or comments given by the prospect due to concerns, fears, confusion, misunderstandings, or unawareness. Objections are advantageous to get because the prospect has trust in you to share them so you can help give clarification or direction.

As salespeople, we have heard numerous objections, such as "the price is too expensive," "I don't have the time," "I'm happy with ABC Company," and so on.

When you first get an objection, you want to

clarify for understanding. Then, you want to empathize with the prospects' feelings about the objection to help them feel at ease and more relaxed. After you empathize, you want to dissect the objection to see if there are other objections in addition to the one(s) verbally expressed.

Finally, you solve the objection(s) using different tactics. Listed below is a detailed explanation on how to solve objections.

Remember that objections are misunderstandings, confusions, fears, and unawareness.

How to Solve Prospect's Concerns/Fears

1. **For Clarity, Question:** Get a clear understanding of their concerns and fears. For example you can say, "How do you mean?"

2. **Empathize:** Empathize with their concerns and fears. "I can understand how you could feel about (concerns/fears). If I were in your shoes, I probably would feel the same way."

3. **Dissect:** "Beside (concerns/fears), is there anything else you are concerned about and that might be holding you back from making a decision to go ahead?"

4. **Solve Concerns/Fears:**

    a) **Bring up their emotional reasons for buying:** In the form of what they are lacking and how you can fill that lack , or what they will gain by using your product (service).

    b) **Question/Resolve:** Their concerns/fears: For example, you can say, "How do you mean?" Why?" Explain how your product (service) can resolve the concerns/fears.

Concerns and Fears

Concern and Fears:

- I don't have the time (telephone concern or fear).

Answer:

- I won't take more than 15 minutes to show you how my product (service) can help you with (benefit to them).

Concerns and Fears:

- I'm not interested.

Answers:

- I guess you're asking if you would enjoy some of our outstanding benefits even though you aren't interested in the overall concept. Is that right?

- Usually when I hear that, it's because you're 100% satisfied with the selling skills of your reps or you've had a bad experience with a third-party trainer.

- The prospect will usually answer with specifics which will give you a genuine selling opportunity. "Do you mind if I ask what you're not interested in?" The prospect will usually answer with specifics which will give you another genuine selling opportunity.

- "I can't expect you to be interested, since I haven't given you much to be interested in" is **not** a good answer because this is the **caller's** information, not the buyer's.

Concerns and Fears:

- I can't afford it.

Answer:

- I believe your real concern is whether the benefits outweigh the initial investment needed, right?

- Why don't we weigh the reasons for going ahead to the reasons for keeping it the way it is to see if the benefits outweigh the investment needed.

Concerns and Fears:

- I got burned on something like this before.

Answer:

- I imagine that you're curious as to how we're structured to avoid the problems usually associated with this kind of situation, correct?

- What questions do you have that I can answer to ease your concerns?

- How can I reassure you so that you're not so concerned?

Concerns and Fears:

- I want to talk it over with...

Answer:

- I understand. If it were up to you alone, would you proceed? If answer is yes, find out what you can do to get their company or other party to buy. See if the prospect can buy without the other party's permission.

Concerns and Fears:

- I want to shop around first.

Answer:

- (Name), we're in agreement that my proposal meets all of the criteria you outlined, at a price you can afford. Why waste your valuable time shopping around, when what you want is right here. Let's get started, OK?

Concerns and Fears:

- I'm happy with ABC Company.

Answers:

- That's great! What is it you like most about ABC?

- Happy to hear that. What things about ABC made you choose them? These answers will give you information on what is important to this company and how you can do better than just match the competition.

  What do you like least?

  If you could improve them in any way, what would that be?

  You have no comparison on service. I suggest you give me a test order, and then judge my service against the best you've had so far.

Concerns and Fears:

- The price is too expensive.

Answers:

- That's an interesting comment. In your own mind, which aspects of my product (service) do you feel are overvalued?

- You know, at times people complain about the price being too expensive. Sometimes it's when they actually make the purchase, but the feeling wears off over time when they realize what a bargain they actually received in terms of quality. Other people complain later if they buy a cheaper product, and wind up having to replace it very quickly. That is when the price really hurts. Let's make sure the latter doesn't happen, OK?

- The dollar price is high, true. But once you see the product you're getting, you'll think it's really inexpensive.

- Which would you rather have: a lower-priced product that may or may not last the year or a high-priced product with the quality guarantees we offer?

- Well, I'm not really sure why your present supplier's price is lower than mine. But, given that price variation, don't you think there must be some kind of difference in what we offer?

- Our price is definitely higher. But you'll get five distinctive features on my product that you won't get anywhere else. Then reiterate the five distinctive features.

- We do charge more, but, we also guarantee same-day order processing. You won't have to wait more than a week to have the goods in your hands.

- Absolutely. We charge more, but we have a reputation for the finest product, quality, and service, and we're very proud of it.

- Reduce the price to its lowest denominator.

Making the Sale

Sale: Making the Sale
 vs. No Sale: Indecision

Now that you have answered all their concerns using additional test closes, it is time to ask for the sale. The sale is done in the following way:

- Make sure that you've answered their concerns and fears.

- Do test closes.

- Ask for the order.

  Examples:

  Well (prospect's name), it looks like we've covered all of the details. What do you suggest we do?

  What do we do from here?

  What is our next step?

Sales Practice

1. Your credibility and company credentials:

2. Finding their emotional reasons to buy:

3. Giving your presentation:

4. Requesting Step (more information and discussion of their concerns, fears, emotions test closes)

5. Asking for the sale:

Name of Prospect _____

Date of Appointment _____

Sales Observations

What did you do right?

1. Your credibility and company credentials:

2. Finding their emotional reasons to buy:

3. Giving your presentation:

4. Requesting Step (more information and discussion of their concerns, fears, emotions test closes)

5. Asking for the sale:

...And, Speaking of Getting
Orders:

A Salesman came back to the

office.

He says to his manager,

"I got 3 Orders."

The manager says,

"Great. What are they?"

The Salesman says,

"Get Out!"

"Stay Out!"

and

"Don't show your

face again!"

Notes

Customer Satisfaction and Ways to Improve Your Profits

In this chapter I will discuss the importance of customer satisfaction and referrals. You will learn:

- How to get satisfied customers and keep them.

- Where and how to ask for quality referrals.

- The way to increase your return on your investment from your current advertising and sales tools.

Customer Service

I have seen sales people spend exorbitant amounts of time and money getting their clients to buy their product or service. Then, after they get the client's business, the client barely ever hears from them unless it is to make another sale.

This is the worst thing you can do because you can lose your client's business. It costs more.

As a business consultant, I make sure that my clients are servicing their customers in a satisfactory manner. I ensure that they are trained to call their customers periodically to see how they're doing, to send items that may be of interest to their customers, and to see if there is anything they can do for the customer to help improve their service.

If a customer is happy with the quality of your product (service), as well as how you service them, they'll be your best form of advertisement — they'll tell their friends and other people they meet, which can bring you more business! You can also feel more comfortable asking them for additional business.

Listed below are some guidelines to ensure customer satisfaction, and some surefire ways to get referrals.

Customer Service: Follow Up

How to Service an Account:

- Call to see how the customer (client) is doing.

- Follow up on any questions asked during call.

- Send any special items of interest from newspapers, bulletins, etc.

- Send customer (client), or tell them, of additional items that could be of benefit to them.

- Have something new to say on every call.

- Make sure that you specify the benefit to the customer (client).

- Speak from genuine interest and sincerity with your customer (client).

- Be honest.

- Follow through on promises made.

- Listen to what they are saying, not what you want to hear.

Referrals

Asking for referrals is a fun way to get more business. It's much easier, more cost-effective, and more efficient than any other means of increasing your sales volume. Listed below is an explanation of ways to get referrals.

Sample Questions for Getting Referrals:

1. "Who do you know who would benefit from my product (service)?"

2. After servicing your customer (client) for a period of time and they specify how pleased they are, you can say, "You've mentioned how pleased you are with my work (customer service). Who else do you know who would be pleased to get the benefits of my product (service) and quality customer service?"

How to Get Referrals:

- Through a networking system
- From a happy client
- From a prospect who doesn't need your service or product.

Measuring Your Advertising and Sales Tools

As you build your business, you will want to use various forms of sales tools and advertising. I have worked with businesses where they have put so much money into advertising and various forms of sales tools and have not measured the results on their investment. They didn't know if they were making a return on their investment or where the most profitable advertising and sales tools were.

Measuring and analyzing where your sales are coming from and what are the most profitable ventures is time consuming. You will be analyzing over a period of time what the most effective sales tools are and why they are effective. This will help you to know in what areas you can improve so that you can become a more effective sales person.

For example, you may be weak on your presentation style or not as effective in answering your customers' (clients') concerns. The result of this is procrastination or no interest. You may realize that your listening and communication skills are not as refined as they could be. You will also know what external factors can be improved. Are you targeting the right location and market? Do you need to update or improve any part of your product or service to make people want to buy?

In addition to measuring and analyzing your sales tools, you also want to measure and analyze your advertising to see how much, if anything, you're getting on your investment. You could be investing in a form of advertising that doesn't target your market, or is being promoted during the wrong hours where the market you want to reach isn't available to hear or see your advertising. It, therefore, becomes an ineffective means of advertising. You could have run the ad during the wrong period of the year resulting in a low amount of calls. For example, an ad you ran during Christmas time brought in a lot of business. Yet, when you ran an ad in the summer, it hardly brought in any business at all. You may think that it was due to where you placed your advertising or that your advertising is not effective any more. Although those could be valid reasons why you didn't get as much business, it could also be because you ran your ad at the wrong time of year.

By measuring your advertising, you will know what form of advertising brings in the most revenue and why. You will also know what form of advertising is unsuccessful and why.

By measuring and analyzing your sales tools, you will be able to see what areas you can improve for better skills, attitudes, goals and self image. You are also able to see what sales tools are the most efficient and which are not and why. This way you can plan:

- When and where to advertise to get your sales;

- How to advertise to get more sales;

- What to advertise;

- Sales tools to use to get more sales;

- Why to use the form of sales tools and advertising you are using that are profitable; and

- Why not to use the form of sales tools and advertising that are not effective.

Types of Sales Tools Used to Bring in Profits

1.   List all of the sales tools that you are using.

2.   List the time invested and dollars spent in each area.

3.   List the most effective to least effective sales tools and why.

Advertising Analysis

1. List below your forms of advertising.

Year 1	Newsletters	Walk-Ins	Yellow Pages	Newspapers	Other	Total Dollars
January						
February						
March						
April						
May						
June						
July						
August						
September						
October						
November						
December						
Notes:						
Year 2						
January						
February						
March						
April						
May						
June						
July						
August						
September						
October						
November						
December						
Notes:						

2. Measure each form of advertising investment with the profits it made to see if you're getting a good return on your investment.

Summary: Analyzing Advertising Return

1. Compare Year 1 with Year 2 to help you make decisions for what revisions, additions, corrections, or changes to make to your advertising budget.

2. What did you learn that would help you improve your profits in Year 3?

Healthy Self Image

Having a healthy self image is important in your endeavors toward greater success. A healthy self image is defined here as "feeling confident about yourself."

Your attitudes, beliefs, communication, and body language reflect the way you feel about yourself. When you have a healthy self image, your attitude is more positive. You take responsibility for your actions and the results of your actions by planning and acting accordingly.

Rather than acting helpless, having self pity, or feeling sorry for yourself, you take care of yourself by honoring your values. Instead of bouncing back and forth between pushing yourself too hard to accomplish something and the other extreme of procrastinating and being unable to act, you make sure your needs and desires are being met.

At the same time, you support others with their challenges and feelings. A healthy self image is not feeling responsible for other peoples' feelings and challenges, trying to resolve them. Nor is it discounting your own feelings, wishes, and desires to please another.

With a healthy self image, you accept, appreciate, and respect yourself and others. You feel worthy and know you deserve only the best. You don't criticize and judge yourself and others.

People with a healthy self image are honest with themselves as they plan their future and then stay in the present, striving toward their accomplishments. They treat themselves and others with genuineness and compassion. They are discerning with situations and people that affect their positive attitudes, well being, and happiness. They also let their personal integrity and intuition be their own guide as they have trust and faith in God or the tool they use in their belief system during their "low times."

With a healthy self image you communicate, using power words such as *could, will, prefer, know, can,* and *choose to* rather than use what I call "slave words" such as *must, need, ought to, think,* and *maybe,* and non-words such as *um, uh, and uh-huh* which show insecurity in yourself.

People with a healthy self image have more erect posture rather than slouchy. They are not sluggish, and refrain from using a tone of voice which is whining or filled with anger or despair.

To conclude, a healthy self image is leading a balanced life both personally and professionally. It's pacing yourself to reach your end results as you stay committed to reaching your dreams and aspirations, while acquiring wisdom and maturity along the way.

Notes

Chapter

7

Tax
Preparation

Tax and License Information

IRS Forms and Publications:

<u>Sole Proprietorship</u> publications: 334, 505, 910

334	Tax guide for small business
505	Tax withholding and estimated tax
910	Guide to tax services
Forms:	1040 ES, 1040, schedule C and SE, 4562, 8829
1040	Income tax form for reporting income, deductions, and credits
1040 ES	Estimated tax for individuals
	Schedule C- Profit or Loss from business
	Schedule SE- Self-Employment tax
4562	Depreciation and amortization
8829	Expenses for business use of your home

<u>Partnership</u> publications: 334, 505, 541, 910

334	Tax guide for small business
505	Tax withholding and estimated tax
541	Tax information for partnerships
910	Guide to tax services
Forms:	1040 ES, 1040, 1065, Schedule K=1, SE, SS-4
1040 ES	Estimated tax for individuals
1065	U. S. Partnership return of income
Schedule SE	Self-Employment tax
Schedule K=1	Partner's share of income, credits, (deductions, etc.)
SS-4	Employer identification number

<u>Corporation</u> publications: 334, 542, 910

334	Tax guide for small business
542	Tax information for corporations
910	Guide to tax services

Form

SS-4	Employer identification number
1120	U.S. Income tax return for Corp.

S. Corporation publications: 15, 589

15	Circular E, Employer's tax guide
589	Tax information for S. Corporations forms: 1120S, SS-4, W-4, 940, 941
1120S	U.S. Income tax return for S. Corporation
SS-4	Employer identification number
W-4	employee fills out for the amount of tax withholdings they're claiming.
940	
FUTA	Federal unemployment
941	
FICA	Social security and medicare taxes

Patents — For inventions. A book entitled, "General Information Concerning Patents," is available for purchase through the U.S. Government Bookstore.

Research on patents can be done in the Patent Depository Library at the University of Washington, Engineering Library (206) 553- 0740.

Copyrights:

For books, manuscripts, and plays. Information on copyright procedures and registration forms may be obtained by calling the Federal Information Center in Portland, OR. 1-800-726-4995.

Trademarks:

For slogans, names, and logo. A booklet entitled, "Basic Facts About Trademarks," is available for purchase through the U.S. Government Bookstore. (703) 557-4357 or (206) 553-4270.

Notes

Bibliography

Books on Selling:

Hopkins, Tom; How to Master the Art of Selling;
Arizona: Tom Hopkins Champions Unlimited,
1982.

Mackay, Harvey; Swim With the Sharks Without
Being Eaten Alive; Chicago: Nightingale-Conant,
1988.

Mueller, Barbara and Vipperman, Carol; Solutions to
Sales Problems; VanCouver: International Self-
Counsel Press, 1982.

Vipperman, Carol; Professional Selling Women's
Guide; VanCouver: International Self-Counsel
Press, 1978.

Whiting, Percy; The 5 Great Rules of Selling; New
York: Dale Carnegie and Associates, 1978.

Books on Building Relationships:

Covey, Stephen R.; 7 Habits of Highly Effective
People; Utah: Covey Leadership Center Inc.,
1991.

Books on Positive Attitudes:

Anderson, U.S.; Three Magic Words; California:
Wilshire Book Co., 1954.

Bach, Marcus; The World of Serendipity; New Jersey:
Prentice-Hall, 1970.

Bryant, Robert; Stop Improving Yourself and Start
Living, California New World Library, 1991.

DeBono, Edward; Six Thinking Hats; Toronto: Key
Porter Books, 1985.

Holmes, Ernest & Kinnear, Willis Hayes; A New
    Design for Living; New Jersey: Prentice-Hall,
    1959.
McWilliams, Peter and Roger, John; You Can't
    Afford the Luxury of a Negative Thought;
    California: Prelude Press, 1988..
Millman, Dan; Secret of the Peaceful Warrior;
    California: H. J. Kramer, Inc., 1991.
Millman, Dan; Way of the Peaceful Warrior; Califor-
    nia: H. J. Kramer, Inc., 1980.
Murphy, Dr Joseph; The Power of Your Subcon-
    scious Mind; New Jersey: Prentice-Hall, 1963.
Roman, Sanaya and Orin; Living With Joy; Califor-
    nia: H. J. Kramer, Inc. 1986.
Seligman, Martin E.P. Ph.D; Learned Optimism;
    New York: A.A. Knopf, 1991.

Notes

Angelica Rose
The Heart Of Motivation
Motivational Speaker & Consultant

Angelica, a business owner since 1984, has been assisting people in enhancing success as a national motivational speaker & consultant. She has done extensive research to find out what it takes to run a successful business and become an effective leader. She has personally turned businesses around as well as interviewed successful businesses and CEO's in 7 states. From Angelica's experience and research, she has come up with proven formulas for enhancing overall success.

Angelica's Unique Buying Advantage is the balance she has with her expertise in the business world coupled with her education and experience in human relations. This includes a bachelors in finance and accounting as well as being a Dale Carnegie Educational Trainer.

Angelica Builds Principal Based Leadership, Heart Centered Values and Overall Success using a unique combination of intuitive, creative and leadership skills.

- Dale Carnegie Trainer/Consultant
- Broadcaster, "Small Business News", on KEZX in Washington
- Produced, an Educational Television Show" in Washington
- Nominated for Mayor's Small Business Award in Washington
- Appeared on numerous talk radio shows and on KIRO Television

* **Increase overall success using 6 proven success formulas**
* **17 ways to communicate more effectively**
* **Enhance SELF directed leadership skills**
* **Improve listening skills using an effective listening technique**
* **Get better results and have FUN doing it using the 4 step approach**
* **Become more relaxed in stressful situations using a visualization technique**
* **Gain more confidence**
* **Build relationships and gain respect through 12 power words**
* **10 Traits of an effective person**
* **Increase client base, customer retention, and profits using the 5 step approach**
* **4 step approach to becoming more promotable**
* **8 common distractions that limit or hold you back and how to minimize them**
* **Run your business more efficiently**
* **Develop 17 ways to improve organizational skills**
AND MORE!

Angelica is a true professional. Her presentation was informative as well as entertaining and should not be missed. I would not hesitate in recommending her to fellow associates & business alike– Dean Cole WAMB

Angelica's style of speaking exemplifies a positive attitude that gives participants the opportunity to relax, interact in a playful way and enhance skill development – Ron Adams Marylhurst University

Angelica was inspiring, motivating, and her ability to bring the group together provided the opportunity to interact between each other professionally and have fun doing it – Linda Bures Washington Association of Student Employment Administrators

Participants are guided through activities and discussions designed to:

* *Experience expressing from the heart*
* *Enhance SELF directed leadership skills*
* *Enhance overall success*

Angelica has developed several topics to choose from as the focus to your experience. These topics can be customized, taken individually or as a series:

Communicate With Confidence *(Keynote 45-90 minutes /Format: Break Out Session 2-3 hours)*

With solid communication and listening skills, relationships are built on solid rock. Through interaction you will learn a proven listening formula, 15 ways to communicate effectively and respond better with others, tips to resolve conflict, and 12 power words to gain confidence and respect.

Sharpen Your Focus To Produce Positive Results *(Keynote 45-90 minutes /Format: Break Out Session 2 hours)*

What ever you stay focused on, you produce those results. Be creative, have fun and learn the power of positive thinking and focused action. You will learn 8 common distractions that limit or hold you back from attaining effective outcomes and ways to minimize them. We will demonstrate how visualization and a mental stimulation exercise helps get better results when making efficient decisions. From this talk you will understand enhance your decision making skills as well as gain a better understanding on handling non-positive circumstances in a positive way.

Soul Inspiration–Awaken Your Inner Success For Complete Fulfillment

(Keynote 45-90 minutes /Format: Break Out Session 2 hours)

Receive 6 proven formulas and techniques on achieving more success: Success Motivators, The Triangle of Success, Cycle of Development, 4 levels of competency and a Proven Definition of Success.

Motivation: Building Productivity *(Format: Break Out Session 2-3 hours)*

Improve organizational skills and become a more effective person as you learn about the 8 common distractions that limit or hold you back from attaining your goals, their effects and 17 ways for effective organization.

Soul Action – How To Awaken Your Leadership Spirit *(Format: Break Out Session 2-3 hours)*

Improve decision making using a 4 step approach and become more relaxed in stressful situations using a visualization technique. You will gain more confidence in your abilities to lead a more balanced lifestyle.

Soul Income – How To Awaken Your Marketing Spirit *(Format: Break Out Session 2-10 hours)*

You will learn 6 proven success formulas that when incorporated will increase your success by multiples. You will learn 4 steps to making yourself more promotable, 16 creative marketing strategies and 2 proven formulas to create a higher demand for the products and/or services you offer. You will leave this talk knowing how to reach your target market, strategic marketing strategies and 10 ways to service your clients more effectively

Living Life As You Always Dreamed It *(Format: Break Out Session 2-10 hours)*

Learn the 8 common distractions that limit and hold you back from attaining your goals and the 8 steps to help you acquire the life you always dreamed. Using visualization, SELF discovery exercises and interaction, you will experience your dreams as reality and recognize those distractions that limit you from acquiring them. You will understand how positive focus empowers as we list and start taking the necessary steps to help manifest the dream in a supportive environment. Please picture clippings, drawing instruments and large a sheet of paper.

Soul Income – How To Awaken Your Sales Spirit *(Format: Break Out Session 2-10 hours)*

Demonstrate value between yourself and potential customers. You will learn how to increase your client base, retain customer loyalty, and improve profitability using the 5 step approach and 10 ways to enhance customer satisfaction. In addition, you will learn 10 ways to be a more effective person and develop better relationship skills.

503-524-4252 8:30-5PM
angelica1rose@yahoo.com   angelica_rose@cheerful.com
http://angelicarose.freeyellow.com/

Products

Secrets To Running A Successful Business $19.95
(How To Have Fun Getting More Business)

Extensive research was done to find out what it takes to run a successful business and become an effective leader. Personally turning businesses around, I have found successful people are effective leaders-*whether you are a sales person, manager, business owner or individual.* In addition, I Interviewed successful businesses and CEO's in 7 states. This book covers *proven* success formulas.

15 Minute Revitalization **Cassette** $10.00

revitalize & receive insights on questions. 15 minutes each side for those on the go.

Articles: $2.00 each 3 or more $1.50

_____ "Mind Map" the way to your goal
_____ Delegating work out: suggestions for making the right decisions
_____ Success through personal & professional development
_____ Keeping your attitude positive during tough times
_____ House of relationships- true meaning of loving relationships
_____ A satisfying career move linked to your worth
_____ Tips to run a successful business
_____ Let a mission statement be your guiding light
_____ A Peaceful Path On Your Journey

Inspirations On Software $14.95

_____ 40 inspirations with pictorials on a 3 1/4 computer disk. When installed you get daily inspiration messages

Prices Do *NOT* include Shipping and Handling.
Please email at *angelica_rose@cheerful.com* **for shipping costs and quantity discounts**

Total Amount Enclosed for Products _____

Motivational Talks
Angelica Rose

_____ Sharpen Your Focus To Produce Positive Results
_____ Communicating With Confidence
_____ Soul Income: How To Awaken Your Sales Spirit
_____ Soul Income: How To Awaken Your Marketing Spirit
_____ Living Life As You Always Dreamed It
_____ Soul Action: How To Awaken Your Leadership Spirit
_____ Motivation: Building Productivity
_____ Soul Inspiration-Awakening Your Inner Success For Complete Fulfillment

_____ **Number of Participants** _____ **Time Length of Talk** _____ **Break Out Session** _____ **Keynote**

Target Audience_____

Location of Talk _____

- -

Name _____ **Company Name** _____

Email Address _____ **Phone Number**_____

Address/City/State/Zip Code _____